WORKBOOK

FOR

Prequel

(A Practical Guide to Rachel Maddow's Book)

An American Fight Against Fascism

Table of Content

Introduction: The United States of America played a vital part in the global war against fascism, which is a pivotal chapter in modern history. In the following conversation, we will investigate the broad topic of the American struggle against fascism, particularly emphasizing the most significant events, persons, and ideas that molded this conflict. Even if we do not have access to some information in Rachel Maddow's book, we are able to present a full summary of this subject by drawing on our knowledge of the past.

I. The Rise of Fascism in Europe

It is vital to explore the historical context of the growth of fascism in Europe during the early 20th century if one is to have any hope of comprehending the American struggle against fascism. This section will provide an overview of the conditions and factors that contributed to the establishment of fascist regimes in countries such as Italy, Germany, and Spain. Examples of these countries are Italy, Germany, and Spain.

II. American Isolationism and Interventionism

In the beginning, the United States responded to the developing fascist movement in Europe by adhering to a policy of isolationism. On the other hand, as the danger posed by fascism grew more obvious, there was a shift in public opinion in the United States. Discuss the debates and political factors that shaped the United States' response to fascism, including the role of people like Charles Lindbergh and the Neutrality Acts.

III. The Spanish Civil War

The worldwide response to fascism was put through its paces during the Spanish Civil War, which took place from 1936 to 1939. The

Abraham Lincoln Brigade, a group of American volunteers, as well as the broader impact of the war on American sentiments toward fascism, should be brought up in the course of the conversation.

IV. World War II and the United States

The United States' approach to conflict changed dramatically after World War II broke out. Discuss the circumstances that led to the United States joining the war, particularly the assault on Pearl Harbor, and emphasize the contributions made by American forces to the overall war effort by the Allies against the Axis countries.

V. The Home Front and Propaganda

Explore the various strategies that the United States government and the media employed to win the American people's support for the war effort. In the fight against fascism, you should talk about the role that propaganda, war bonds, and the mobilization of industry played.

VI. Prominent American Figures Who Fight Against Fascism

The names of important people who played vital roles in the fight against fascism should be highlighted, such as Franklin D. Roosevelt, Dwight D. Eisenhower, and Eleanor Roosevelt. Have a conversation on how they contributed to the war effort and how they helped rebuild Europe after the war.

VII. The Nuremberg Trials and the United Nations

Explore the postwar efforts, represented by the Nuremberg Trials, to make Nazi officials accountable for the crimes they committed during the war. Talk about how the United Nations came to be and the role it plays in encouraging international collaboration and reducing the likelihood of future conflicts.

VIII. The Legacy of the American Fight Against Fascism

Consider the long-lasting effects that World War II and the fight against fascism had on American society as well as the geopolitical landscape of the world. Discuss the beginning of the Cold War and the subsequent partitioning of Europe, as well as the rise of the civil rights movement and the search for social justice in the United States.

IX. Contemporary Relevance

Make comparisons between the fight against fascism in the 20th century and the struggles we now face regarding authoritarianism, extremism, and human rights. Let's have a conversation on the things we can take away from the American experience in the fight against fascism.

Conclusion: The struggle of the United States of America against fascism was a convoluted and multidimensional conflict that lasted for decades and had far-reaching repercussions. It profoundly altered the United States' place in the world, put the nation's dedication to democratic principles to the test, and created a legacy that continues to have an impact on international affairs. This conversation provides a broad framework for understanding the historical background and significance of the American fight against fascism. While we wait for further details on Rachel Maddow's book, we may take advantage of this framework.

Chapter 1: The Origins of Fascism

This chapter will dig deeply into the beginnings of fascism, investigating its ideological foundations and manifestations around the world. Maddow would most likely explain how fascism arose as a reaction to perceived societal decadence and instability after World War I, specifically in Italy under Benito Mussolini and then in Germany under Adolf Hitler.

Maddow might dive into fascism's key ideas, such as nationalist and authoritarian ideals, dissent repression, and vilification of perceived 'otherness.' This research could be supplemented with extensive analyses of the sociopolitical environments in which these ideas took root and thrived.

Chapter 2: American Involvement in WWII

The second chapter might address the gradual transformation in American isolationist policy throughout the early stages of World War II, culminating in full military engagement following the Pearl Harbor assault. Maddow might highlight the courage and sacrifice of the American soldiers, together with Allied forces, in the face of Nazi invasion.

The societal and political developments that occurred in the United States during this time period would almost certainly be a focus topic. Maddow may also delve into the paradox of America's struggle against fascism abroad while coping with racial segregation and inequality at home, emphasizing figures such as the Tuskegee Airmen who fought heroically for a country that did not provide them equal rights.

Chapter 3: The Cold War and Ideological Conflicts

This chapter would most likely trace the transition from World War II to the Cold War, when ideological warfare moved from fascism to communism. Maddow may juxtapose America's fight against fascist authoritarianism with its attitude to communist governments, looking at occasions where the US assisted authoritarian regimes in order to limit communist spread.

This era's ideological and geopolitical disputes will be painstakingly examined, with a focus on how these historical events affected America's position on democracy, freedom, and human rights. McCarthyism's growth and fall, the Cuban Missile Crisis, and the Vietnam War might all serve as illustrative examples of the complexity inherent in America's Cold War ideological fights.

Historical Context Reflections

Maddow would most likely synthesize these historical accounts at the end of this segment to show how the American fight against fascism has been connected with the country's broader intellectual, political, and moral history. The investigation of America's historical backdrop would seek to offer readers a fundamental knowledge of how the country has navigated, faced, and sometimes paradoxically interacted with fascist beliefs.

This theoretical account would most likely highlight Rachel Maddow's well-known tendency for meticulous study and in-depth analysis, providing a multifaceted view of America's historical path in its confrontations with fascism. She would most likely draw connections between historical events and current events, implicitly implying that learning history is critical in detecting and responding to modern versions of extremism and authoritarianism.

- **America's response to the rise of fascism in the early 20th century.**

In the early twentieth century, America's response to the emergence of fascism was marked by a complex combination of isolationism, economic cooperation, and eventual military participation. This reaction occurred within a larger global environment defined by the aftermath of World War I, the Great Depression, and, finally, World War II.

Economic Interests and Isolationism: Following World War I, the United States pursued a mostly isolationist foreign policy. The tragedies of World War I had instilled in Americans a strong desire to avoid being involved in European conflicts. The United States was more concerned with its own economic recovery and progress, and there was a strong reluctance to intervene in what were perceived as "Old World" concerns.

This isolationism, however, coexisted with economic objectives. American corporations and banks had strong economic ties with fascist regimes. Corporations, for example, continued to deal with and operate in fascist-led countries, prioritizing economic interests and stability over ideological resistance.

The Spanish Civil War: The Spanish Civil War (1936-1939) was an early example of open opposition to fascism. Thousands of Americans volunteered to fight as members of the International Brigades against Francisco Franco's fascist forces. While this was not an official American government intervention, it demonstrated that a part of the populace recognized and opposed the fascist threat.

Official Reaction and Policy Change: As the Axis nations, particularly Nazi Germany, expanded their territory, America's official response began to evolve. When World War II broke out in 1939, it sparked controversy in the United States about its involvement in the battle. Recognizing the threat posed by fascism, President Franklin D. Roosevelt sought to strengthen Allied nations through measures such as the Lend-Lease Act, which provided material assistance to countries fighting the Axis powers.

Pearl Harbor and Full-Scale Intervention: Following the attack on Pearl Harbor on December 7, 1941, the United States was forced to intervene militarily. This act of aggression by Imperial Japan, an Axis state, forced the United States to declare war. Once committed, the United States was critical in defeating the Axis forces in both the European and Pacific theaters.

Implications for Society: The fight against fascism had far-reaching social consequences in the United States. The conflict sparked substantial societal changes, such as the desegregation of the military forces and improved possibilities for women in the labor force. It also highlighted sharp contrasts, as a government opposing fascist ideology overseas maintained racially discriminatory policies at home, as epitomized by the internment of Japanese Americans.

Conclusion: The recognition of the harm that fascist doctrines and regimes posed to global security and democratic norms overcame America's early reluctance to engage in the struggle against fascism. The eventual US military participation was critical in the downfall of fascist regimes in Europe and Asia. The early twentieth-century experiences served as critical lessons in international relations and policymaking, molding American foreign policy and its postwar stance against authoritarianism and totalitarianism.

The interaction and battle with fascism during this period would be considered as a moral and ideological endeavor, stimulating discussions and reflections on the values and principles that characterize American civilization.

- **A historical review of fascism, with a focus on Mussolini's Italy and Hitler's Germany**

Fascism: A Historical Overview: Fascism is a far-right, authoritarian ultranationalism marked by dictatorial authority, strong nationalist passion, and, in many cases, bigotry. It first appeared in the early twentieth century, most notably in Italy and Germany, respectively, under the leadership of Benito Mussolini and Adolf Hitler.

Mussolini's Italy

Rise of Fascism:

Origins: Fascism in Italy began in the tumultuous years after World War I. Former socialist Benito Mussolini created the Fascist Party in 1919. Disillusioned war veterans, nationalists, and those fearful of communist revolution backed the party.

March on Rome: In 1922, Mussolini and his Blackshirts marched on Rome, prompting King Victor Emmanuel III to name Mussolini as Prime Minister. Mussolini then steadily undermined Italy's democratic institutions, establishing a totalitarian state in its place.

Policies and Ideology:

Authoritarianism: Mussolini's rule was distinguished by the suppression of political dissent, rigorous governmental control, and a cult of personality. Mussolini fostered the notion of "Il Duce" - the leader to whom everyone owed total fealty.

Nationalism: The concepts of national rebirth and extreme nationalism were important to Italian Fascism. Territorial expansionism resulted in the invasions of Ethiopia and Albania.

Corporatism: Mussolini created a corporatist economic structure in an attempt to reconcile class disputes and create a peaceful national society.

Impact:

Mussolini's administration left a legacy of ruthless repression, economic insecurity, and military adventure, all of which contributed to Italy's defeat in WWII.

Hitler's Germany

The Rise of Fascism:

Origins: In part influenced by Mussolini, Adolf Hitler converted the German Workers' Party into the National Socialist German Workers' Party (Nazi Party). The Nazis acquired support by capitalizing on the economic problems and national humiliation caused by the Treaty of Versailles.

Seizure of Power: Hitler was chosen Chancellor by President Paul von Hindenburg in 1933. Hitler quickly cemented power, eliminating criticism and establishing a totalitarian regime.

Policies and Ideology:

Racism and anti-Semitism: Racist ideologies that defined non-Aryans as inferior were central to Nazi philosophy. This resulted in the systematic slaughter of six million Jews, as well as Roma, disabled persons, Poles, Soviets, homosexuals, and others, during the Holocaust.

Lebensraum: Nazi ideology emphasized the necessity for living space, which led to aggressive territorial expansion and invasions of several European countries.

Totalitarianism: Hitler's dictatorship maintained strict and pervasive control over all parts of life, enforcing compliance and suppressing resistance through propaganda, mass surveillance, and the SS.

Impact:

Hitler's goal of racial purity and geographical expansion sparked WWII, resulting in enormous misery, loss of life, and destruction. The revelation of the Holocaust's horrors prompted a global reckoning with the atrocities perpetrated and transformed international conventions, resulting in the formation of the United Nations and the Universal Declaration of Human Rights.

Comparative Analysis

While Mussolini's Italy and Hitler's Germany differed in ideological intricacies and application of fascist ideals, they shared basic fascist elements: dictatorial authority, intense nationalism, repression of dissent, and a dedication to territorial expansion. The rise, manifestation, and eventual defeat of fascism in these countries are significant chapters in the history of the twentieth century, teaching us about the risks of unbridled authoritarianism and the importance of preserving democratic norms.

I. The Rise of Fascism in Europe

Introduction: The development of fascism in Europe in the early twentieth century set the ground for a global battle that would fundamentally impact world history. This section will look at the situations, factors, and ideologies that led to the rise of fascist regimes in nations such as Italy, Germany, and Spain.

1. *Historical Background*

• Begin by offering a quick review of Europe's post-World War I political, economic, and social context.

2. Contributing Factors to Fascism • Identify and describe the primary elements that propelled Europe's emergence of fascism. Economic insecurity, political divisiveness, and the aftermath of the Treaty of Versailles may be among these concerns.

3. Important People and Movements

• Highlight key personalities and movements linked with the advent of fascism, such as Italy's Benito Mussolini and Germany's Adolf Hitler. Give a brief biographical overview and discuss their ideologies.

4. *Ideological Underpinnings*

• Delve deeper into fascism's ideological foundations, such as authoritarianism, nationalism, and militarism. Explain how these ideas influenced the European populace.

5. *The Spread of Fascism*

• Describe fascism's geographical spread in Europe, highlighting its spread from Italy and Germany to other countries such as Austria, Hungary, and Spain.

6. *Democracy's Threats*

• Discuss how the advent of fascism posed serious threats to Europe's democratic institutions and norms. Mention civil freedoms degradation, censorship, and opposition suppression.

7. The Function of Propaganda

• Investigate the function of propaganda in the propagation of fascist ideology and the formation of public opinion. Give examples of propaganda items and their effectiveness.

8. Racism and anti-Semitism

• Address anti-Semitism and racism in fascist regimes, especially in Nazi Germany. Describe how these ideas resulted in persecution and genocide.

9. Crisis Points That Lead to War • Conclude this section by analyzing the key events that heightened tensions in Europe and ultimately led to World War II.

Conclusion: Summarize the important arguments raised in this part, emphasizing the importance of understanding fascism's emergence in Europe as a precursor to the greater battle and the American fight against fascism.

II. American Isolationism and Interventionism

Introduction: The stance of the United States on the advent of fascism in Europe was distinguished by a complicated interplay of isolationism and interventionism. This section will look at how American views and policies changed throughout this key period.

1. Separatism vs. Interventionism

• Begin by defining isolationism and interventionism in the context of US foreign policy. Examine the historical origins of these beliefs.

2. Isolationism in Early America

• Explain the United States' initial non-interventionist position in European affairs throughout the early phases of fascism's growth. Emphasize the need to avoid "entangling alliances."

3. Deliberations and Political Dynamics

• Investigate the political arguments and forces that created American perceptions toward fascism. Mention key personalities and groups on both sides, such as America First and its opponents.

4. The Acts of Neutrality

• Describe the succession of Neutrality Acts passed by the United States Congress in the 1930s. Discuss their goal and the implications for US foreign policy.

5. Events that Tested Isolationism

• Describe major international and domestic events and changes that undermined American isolationism, such as the Spanish Civil War and the escalating aggression of Axis countries.

6. Transition to Interventionism

• Describe the elements that gradually altered public opinion in the United States toward interventionism. Including events such as the French Revolution, the Battle of Britain, and the Tripartite Pact.

7. The Attack on Pearl Harbor and the Beginning of World War II

• Discuss the key event of the December 1941 attack on Pearl Harbor and its importance in compelling the United States to engage in World War II.

8. Democracy's Arsenal

• Define the term "Arsenal of Democracy," as coined by President Franklin D. Roosevelt, and its significance in assisting the Allies.

9. The Function of American Diplomacy

• Highlight the United States diplomatic attempts to forge alliances and coordinate the war effort against fascism, such as the Lend-Lease Act and the Atlantic Charter.

Conclusion: Summarize the important arguments raised in this part, emphasizing how the change from isolationism to interventionism constituted a watershed moment in American foreign policy and the battle against fascism.

In this part of Rachel Maddow's hypothetical book "An American Fight Against Fascism" will focus on modern forms of fascism, demonstrating how traces of fascist ideology pervade contemporary political and socioeconomic landscapes, notably in the United States.

- **Fascism and Contemporary American Politics**

Extremist Organizations and Ideologies:

Maddow would very certainly discuss the return of extremist groups in the United States, as well as the beliefs they promote. The chapter might examine how these groups are influenced by past fascist ideologies like racial superiority, authoritarianism, and anti-democratic values, and how they have found new life in the digital era via online forums and social media platforms.

Polarization and Political Rhetoric:

Maddow may go into the current political climate in the United States, looking at how fascist rhetoric has penetrated mainstream political discourse. The contentious and politicized aspect of modern American politics may be addressed, with an emphasis on how it fosters radical beliefs.

- ## Socioeconomic Factors

Economic Inequality and Social Inequality:

This chapter could look at how economic gaps and social inequality can fuel fascist ideology. Maddow may investigate how economic insecurity and a sense of loss of status can contribute to the scapegoating of minority groups and a desire for authoritarian leadership.

Examples of Case Studies:

Maddow may dig into particular case studies that demonstrate how nations, including America, have historically responded to these forces. Economic crises, racial conflicts, and perceived threats to national identity might all be examined in depth, revealing how they lead to the emergence of authoritarian principles.

- ## The Role of the Media

The Media and Extremism Propagation:

The function of the media in the spread or suppression of extremist beliefs will be a critical topic in this section. Maddow could investigate how conventional and digital media can be utilized to promote, mainstream, or combat fascist ideology, as well as how they influence public opinion and political discourse.

Misinformation and deception:

Maddow might investigate the spread of misinformation and deception in the digital age, as well as the effects on democratic cultures. She may talk about how the spread of inaccurate or misleading information can undermine trust in institutions, exacerbate societal differences, and fuel extremist ideologies.

Reflections on Contemporary Manifestations:

Maddow would most likely conclude this section by reflecting on the ramifications of current fascism for American democracy and society. The investigation would most likely include a multidimensional exploration of the sociopolitical environment, demonstrating how the shadows of fascist ideology persist in the modern world.

The comparison of historical fascism and its present incarnations would highlight the ongoing risks to democratic norms and the need for continuing vigilance, education, and active resistance to the return of authoritarian ideals in the twenty-first century.

PROMINENT AMERICAN FIGURES IN THE FIGHT AGAINST FASCISM AND THE LEGACY OF THE AMERICAN FIGHT AGAINST FASCISM

Introduction: Several notable figures arose throughout the American battle against fascism, each contributing significantly to the efforts against Axis powers. This section will look into these notable people's lives and contributions.

1. Franklin D. Roosevelt (FDR)

• Begin with a primer on Franklin D. Roosevelt, President of the United States for the majority of World War II.

• Discuss FDR's leadership style and the policies he put in place to help the war effort.

• Highlight key moments during his administration, such as his "Four Freedoms" address and the signing of the Atlantic Charter.

2. Dwight D. Eisenhower

• Discuss Dwight D. Eisenhower, a notable military leader during World War II.

• Talk about his role as Supreme Commander of the Allied Expeditionary Force in Europe and his role in the D-Day invasion.

• Mention his later role as the United States' 34th President.

3. Eleanor Roosevelt

• Investigate Eleanor Roosevelt's contributions as First Lady during FDR's term.

• Highlight her human rights advocacy and work on the Universal Declaration of Human Rights at the United Nations.

4. Douglas MacArthur

• Introduce General Douglas MacArthur, a prominent military leader in World War II's Pacific Theater.

• Talk about his memorable return to the Philippines and his involvement in Japan's postwar occupation.

5. George S. Patton

• Explain General George S. Patton was a well-known leader in the European Theater.

• Talk about his most important campaigns and methods, as well as his complex personality.

6. Harry S. Truman

• Present Harry S. Truman, who took over as President after FDR and made important decisions at the conclusion of WWII.

• Emphasize Truman's role in the decision to drop nuclear weapons on Hiroshima and Nagasaki.

7. George C. Marshall

• Go over General During World War II, George C. Marshall was the Chief of Staff of the United States Army.

• Describe his contributions to military strategy and his role in the Marshall Plan for European reconstruction after the war.

8. Eleanor Roosevelt

• Discuss Eleanor Roosevelt's continued influence after FDR's administration, particularly her role in the United Nations and human rights advocacy.

9. Other Notable Individuals

• Mention other famous personalities who helped the United States resist fascism, such as Winston Churchill, a close ally, and Thomas E. Dewey, who ran against FDR in the 1944 presidential election.

Conclusion: Summarize the essential roles that these prominent American figures played in the struggle against fascism, both militarily and diplomatically. In this vital moment, emphasize how their leadership and contributions affected the direction of history.

The Legacy of the American Fight Against Fascism

Introduction: The American war against fascism in the twentieth century had far-reaching and long-lasting consequences for both the United States and the rest of the globe. In this section, we shall look at the struggle's lasting legacy and its impact on different elements of society and geopolitics.

1. American Power Transformation

• Begin by discussing how America's participation in World War II changed the country into a superpower.

• Explain how the United States and the Soviet Union emerged as the two dominant global powers, resulting in the Cold War.

2. International Cooperation and the United Nations

• Emphasize the United Nations (UN) role in encouraging international collaboration and preventing future crises.

• Discuss the founding of the United Nations, the principles of the UN Charter, and its current relevance.

3. European Reconstruction and the Marshall Plan

• Learn about the Marshall Plan, an American effort that gave economic assistance to rebuild war-torn Europe.

• Discuss how this approach helped Western Europe recover and prevented communism from spreading.

4. Accountability and the Nuremberg Trials

• Consider the significance of the Nuremberg Trials in making Nazi officials accountable for war crimes.

• Discuss how the principles of international law developed during the trials continue to influence war crimes prosecutions today.

5. The Civil Rights Movement

• Investigate the relationship between the fight against fascism and the American civil rights movement.

• Emphasize how African American soldiers returning from WWII aided the civil rights movement.

6. The Universal Declaration of Human Rights and Human Rights

• Examine the relationship between the fight against fascism and the postwar emphasis on human rights.

• Describe the origins of the Universal Declaration of Human Rights and its continuing importance in advancing individual liberties.

7. The Cold War and Europe's Divisions

• Examine the Cold War's legacy and the split of Europe into Eastern and Western blocs.

• Explain how this geopolitical conflict influenced global politics for decades and led to proxy wars.

8. Current Importance

• Draw parallels between the American struggle against fascism and current challenges, such as the spread of authoritarianism and radical ideologies.

• Discuss how the lessons learned from the twentieth-century fight against fascism can be applied to modern international relations.

9. The Struggle for Peace and Diplomacy

• Highlight the value of diplomacy and nonviolent conflict settlement as lessons from the fight against fascism.

• Highlight diplomatic efforts, arms control treaties, and peacekeeping missions that are helping to maintain global stability.

Conclusion: Summarize the lasting legacy of America's war against fascism, highlighting how it shaped modern world order, influenced civil rights movements, and continues to give essential lessons for resolving contemporary difficulties in the search for

Historical Antifascist Movements

Alliances in World War II:

Maddow could begin by recounting the historical alliances formed during World War II to combat fascist regimes. She might detail the military strategies and the ideological campaigns developed by the Allies to counteract the Axis powers, discussing the roles of nations, leaders, and ordinary citizens.

Post-War Institutions:

This chapter could also look at the postwar organizations, treaties, and standards put in place to prevent fascism from resurfacing and to promote international peace, security, and human rights, such as the United Nations and the Universal Declaration of Human Rights.

Contemporary Resistance

Antifascist Activism:

Maddow would likely delve into contemporary antifascist movements and activism, detailing their goals, methods, and impact. She may discuss the underlying values of the antifascist movement, demonstrating how they are rooted in a dedication to equality, justice, and opposition to authoritarianism and racism.

Legislative and Policy Actions:

This chapter could also look at the role of legislation and policy in combating extremism and authoritarianism. Maddow could explore the balance between maintaining democratic freedoms and principles and tackling challenges to national security, social peace, and democratic governance.

The Role of Education and Civil Society

Educational Initiatives:

Maddow could discuss the paramount importance of education in fostering democratic values, critical thinking, and tolerance. She can highlight activities and programs aimed at teaching the public about the history of fascism and the worth of democratic ideals.

Civil Society and Community Participation:

This chapter would likely emphasize the significance of civil society groups and community engagement in fighting fascist beliefs. Maddow might look into how grassroots movements, community dialogues, and civic education can help cultivate an informed and resilient population capable of opposing authoritarian impulses.

Reflections on the Anti-Fascist Struggle:

In completing this portion, Maddow would likely integrate the numerous lines of resistance against fascism, commenting on the lessons learned and the problems ahead. She may underscore the ongoing importance of the battle against fascism, emphasizing the necessity for vigilance, education, and active participation to protect democratic institutions and values from authoritarian assault.

Maddow may emphasize that the fight against fascism is not limited to battlefields or moments of acute crises, but is a long-term endeavor requiring the dedication of individuals, communities, and nations to the principles of democracy, equality, and justice.

Made in United States
Troutdale, OR
11/27/2023